SCIENCE IN OUR

SHAPES
and
STRUCTURES

Contributory Author
Brian Knapp, BSc, PhD
Art Director
Duncan McCrae
Special photography
Graham Servante
Special models
Tim Fulford, Head of CDT, Leighton Park School
Editorial consultants
Anna Grayson, Rita Owen
Science advisor
Jack Brettle, BSc, PhD, Chief Research Scientist, Pilkington plc
Production controller
Gillian Gatehouse
Print consultants
Landmark Production Consultants Ltd
Printed and bound in Hong Kong

Designed and produced by EARTHSCAPE EDITIONS

First published in the United Kingdom in 1991
by Atlantic Europe Publishing Company Ltd,
86 Peppard Road, Sonning Common, Reading,
Berkshire, RG4 9RP

Copyright © 1991
Atlantic Europe Publishing Company Ltd

British Library Cataloguing in Publication Data

Knapp, Brian
  Shapes and Structures
  1. Geometry – For children
  I. Title   II. Series
  516
         ISBN 1-869860-80-2

All rights reserved. No part of this publication may be reproduced, stored in a retrieval system, or transmitted in any form or by any means otherwise, without prior permission in writing of the publisher, nor be otherwise circulated in any form of binding or cover other than that in which it is published and without a similar condition including this condition being imposed on the subsequent purchaser.

In this book you will find some words that have been shown in **bold** type. There is a full explanation of each of these words on pages 46 and 47.

On many pages you will find experiments that you might like to try for yourself. They have been put in a coloured box like this.

Acknowledgements
The publishers would like to thank the following:
Andrew Burnett, Leighton Park School,
Micklands Primary School, Oxford University Museum, Redlands County Primary School, Reading University Geology Department and The Goldfish Bowl

Picture credits
t=top b= bottom l=left r=right

All photographs from the Earthscape Editions photographic library except the following:
Hutchison Library 11; ZEFA 6, 8, 23

Contents

Introduction	Page 4
Pyramids and wedges	6
Blocks	8
Curves	10
Crinkles	12
Arches	14
Columns	16
Bars and beams	18
Tubes	20
Hanging cables	22
Tight wires	24
Cones	26
Dishes and domes	28
Spheres	30
Shells	32
Getting support	34
How frames work	36
Nests	38
Packed together	40
Skyscrapers	42
Our strong shapes	44
New words	46
Index	48

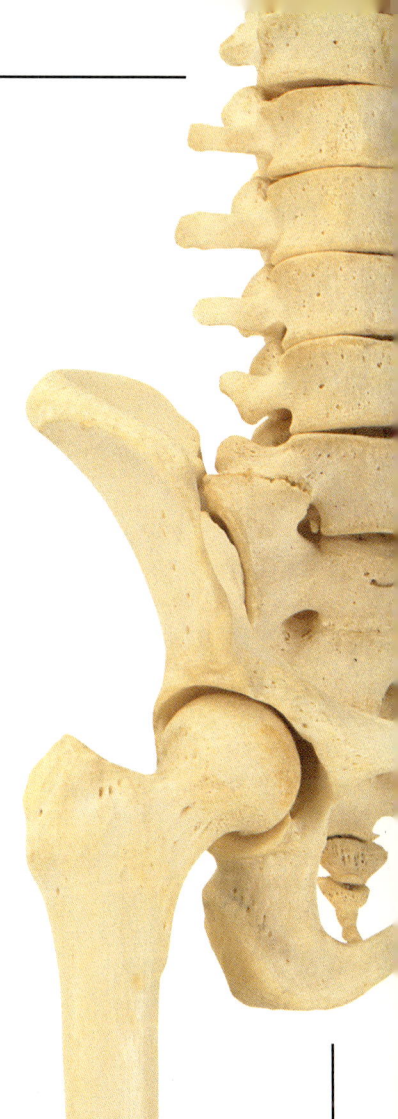

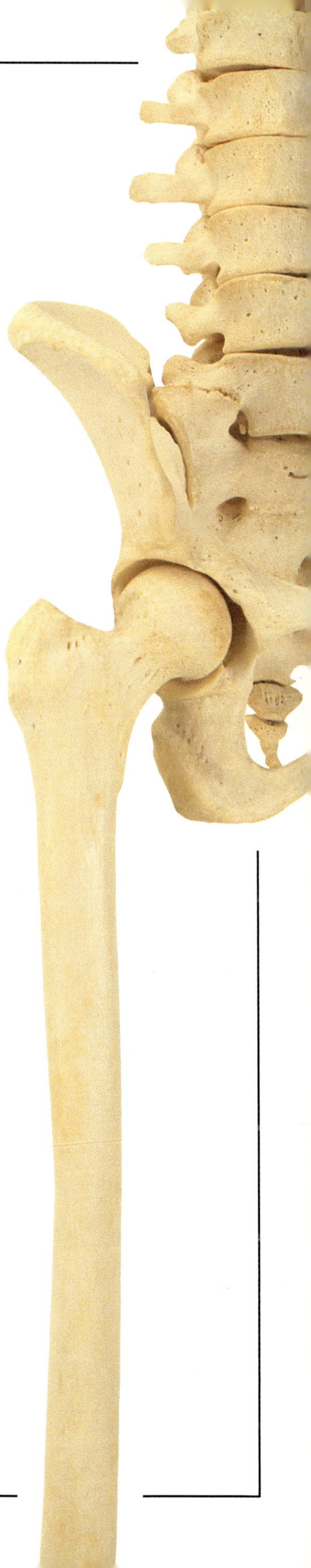

Introduction

nests
page 38

shells
page 32

skyscrapers
page 42

spokes
page 24

blocks
page 8

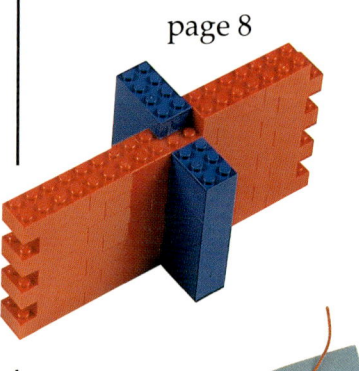

Look at the room you are sitting in. You will see a wide variety of shapes that are strong enough to be pulled, squashed, bent, twisted, hit or dropped.

The walls of your room may be made of building blocks, stacked together. Each block has an oblong or **rectangular**, shape.

Your body has to be made of strong shapes as well. Feel your arms and legs. They are long and round, similar to **rods**, or **cylinders**. Now feel your head. It is round in every direction– roughly ball-shaped or a **sphere**.

A **pyramid** was the strong shape the

skeletons
page 44

crinkles
page 12

columns
page 16

towers
page 20

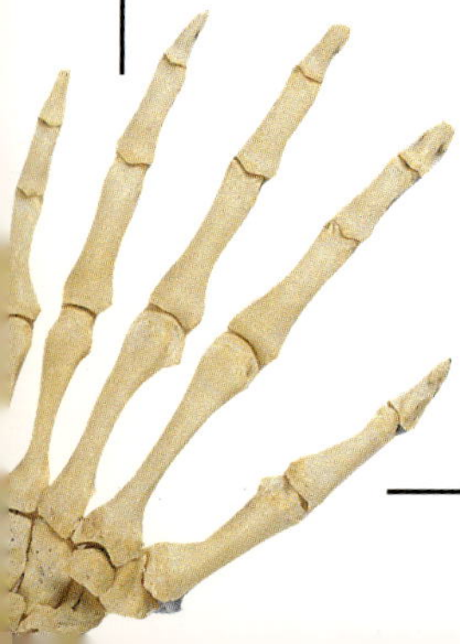

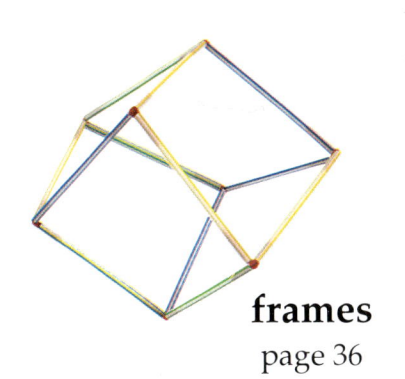

beams
page 18

domes
page 28

wedges
page 6

frames
page 36

arches
page 14

ancient Egyptians used to build their famous burial chambers. **Cones** are strong shapes, too. Look at the sharp ends of needles, for example.

Our world is exciting because the mix of shapes *and* materials is almost endless. In this book you will see a wide variety of interesting shapes. Some are made with everyday materials, others with very special materials. Some of the strongest shapes are made by nature, others by the clever skills of engineers.

Strong shapes are all around you, so there is plenty to look out for. Just turn to a page and start your investigations.

bridges
page 22

spheres
page 30

curves
page 10

cones
page 26

honeycombs
page 40

props
page 34

Pyramids and wedges

Some shapes are wider at the bottom than the top. This is called tapering.

A tapering shape on its side is a wedge. It can be used to force even giant blocks apart.

Triangular test
Wedges and pyramids are examples of a triangular shape that can stand up to great **forces**. It has been used in the design of the **skyscraper** shown in the picture above.

The great pyramids
A pyramid is a shape that has triangular sides meeting in a point. The great pyramids of Giza in Egypt (see picture below) are tombs for kings (pharaohs) that were built by the Ancient Egyptians over 3000 years ago.

The builders of the pyramids found out about strong shapes by trial and error. At first they built a pyramid with steeply sloping sides. They found that this kept falling down.

Having learned this lesson they built pyramids with less steep sides.

Make a door stop
A wedge is a tapering shape that makes a good kind of doorstop. Ask a grown-up to saw a piece of wood to give several wedge shapes like the ones shown below.

Try each wedge in turn to see which one is best at holding a door open. When you have found the one that works best, compare it with a doorstop that can be bought in a shop. Are the shapes similar?

A wedge sold in a shop

Opening wedges
Wedges are good at prising things apart because they have a thin blade at one end which changes to a thick blade at the other. You can see a wedge-shape at the end of this chisel. It is used for making a cut in wood.

7

Blocks

A block is a simple rectangular shape where all the sides are at right angles to one another.

Building blocks and boxes are common examples of a rectangular shape.

Rectangular shapes are easy to stack. However, the strength of a stack of blocks is helped by the pattern of stacking as well as the shape of the blocks.

Easy transport
Rectangular boxes of the same size are easy to transport. This is the reason awkward shapes are often packed into cases before they are transported.

One of the most common types of box is the steel container. Containers are the same shape and size throughout the world. A manufacturer packs his product into the container at the factory; it is then lifted onto a truck and taken away. It can be loaded onto a railway wagon or stacked on a ship and lifted back on to a truck with equal ease.

This is the Great Wall of China, a fortification made of bricks that has lasted three thousand years

Strength in the dents

Some building blocks have dents in their top and bottom faces. This is the place filled by **mortar**. Here the mortar acts just like the pegs on the model building blocks shown in the picture below. It stops the blocks from sliding over one another and makes the wall stronger.

The dent on this block is designed to take mortar. The mortar shows between lines of blocks on most walls

Design a wall

Make a wall using model building blocks like the one shown in this picture. See how tall the wall can be before it starts to wobble. Now think of ways of making it wobble less. One way is to add thicker wall pieces called **piers**. They are shown in this picture.

Another way is to make all parts of the wall thicker, but this would use more blocks. Try to find the tallest wall that will not fall down by using as few blocks as possible.

Wall

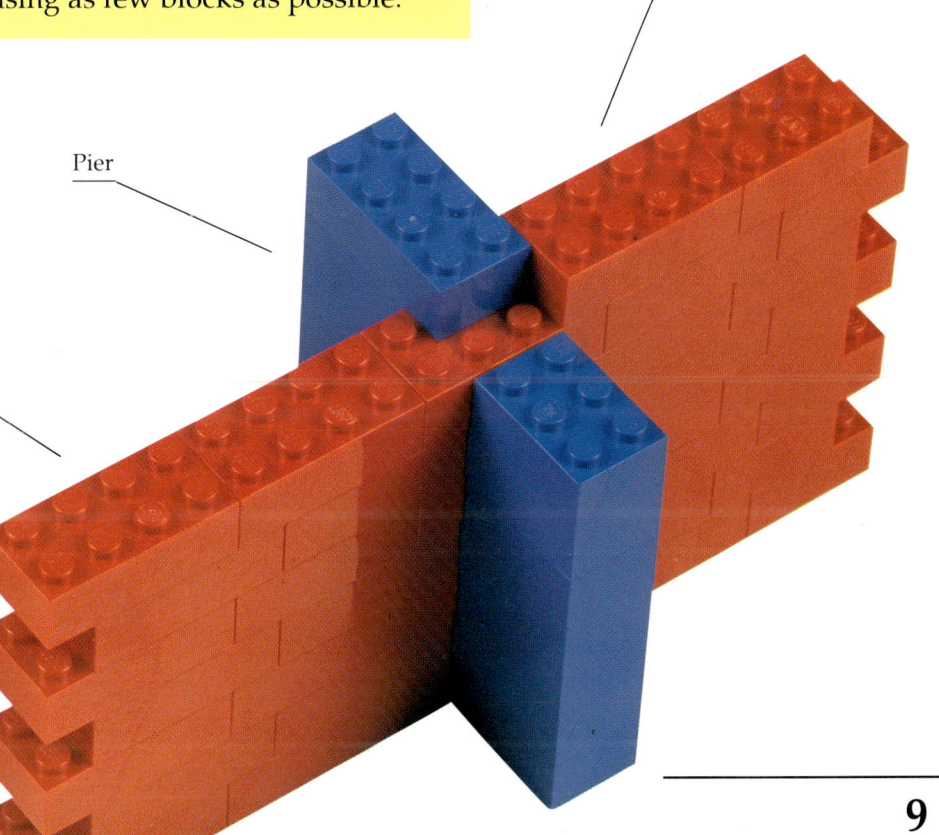

Pier

Overlapping layers of blocks

9

Curves

Have you ever wondered why many shapes are curved? Curved shapes can be made very light and yet very strong. This saves on materials and it is widely used in nature and by engineers.

The use of curved shapes allows an engineer to build a strong structure with thin sheets of metal and plastic. This saves money and energy.

You can find many other examples in everyday life.

Petals
As flowers stand out from the plant they are often exposed to buffeting by strong winds. Although petals may be thinner than paper they are strong because they are curved.

Strong sheet
A flat sheet of material will bend and flop about. Try taking a sheet of paper and hold it by one side. Now try lifting it by the side. It will soon flop over.

Now start again. This time make the paper slightly curved and lift it above your head. This time the paper will feel rigid. You have made a stronger shape.

Roofs

These beautifully shaped roofs on houses in Indonesia show how curves can be used to make lightweight bamboo frames very strong. Without the use of curved shapes the front parts of these roofs would need to be supported by cumbersome pillars.

Pop a curve

A curved piece of material will hold its shape very well. If you take an empty curved plastic bottle and press it gently then let go, it will pop back into shape. But if you press it so that it goes past the 'flat' stage, it will pop into a new curve – a dent – and keep this shape.

Petals have to stand up to insects landing and taking off in their search for **nectar**

11

Crinkles

One way of adding strength to a structure is by adding a crinkle – or **corrugation**.

A crinkle is a curve that is so tight it cannot change shape when it is pressed. This makes it more useful than a curved sheet when extra strength is needed in one direction.

Natural support
Cacti often have specially shaped stems that are covered with corrugations. The corrugations help to support the fleshy stem of the tall saguaro cactus from Arizona USA shown here. This cactus is three metres tall.

Stronger can
This can is made of thin metal, but it will crush if pushed hard from the side. To make the shape stronger and more rigid the can has been pressed into corrugations. This adds strength with hardly any increase in weight.

Concertina paper

Corrugated paper is found in many packs to protect the things inside.

You can find out about corrugations by using a sheet of plain paper. Make a series of small holes in a line about 5 centimetres apart using a pointed object such as a knitting needle.

Next, thread a piece of string through the holes, going alternately over and under the paper. Make a big knot at one end. Then pull the string and the paper will go into corrugations. Fix the free end with a knot to keep the corrugations in place.

Find out how the corrugated paper behaves. Can you stand it on end? If you tighten the crinkles by shortening the string does this make the paper stronger or weaker?

Good protection
Many shells have crinkly shapes. This helps the shell to survive against buffeting waves.

Arches

An arch is a curve that supports material above an opening. Natural arches in cliffs and caves support thousands of tonnes of rock.

The shape is so strong that arches are used to hold up huge bridges and to provide openings in buildings.

Natural arch
There are many natural stone arches in the world. Most of them are found along coasts, where the cliffs are battered by the sea.

Sometimes arches also form in inland cliffs such as here at Utah, USA. Rainstorms over thousands of years have carried away the sand grains from the middle of the cliffs. But the grains in the top layer of rock have resisted the attack.

Look carefully at the picture above and you will see a person standing inside this arch.

The first iron bridge
The first iron bridge was built to span the River Severn at Ironbridge in England. See how the arch is made of long curved bars that carry the weight of the roadway.

An arch with **key stones**

These blocks are screwed to the base to hold the arch in place

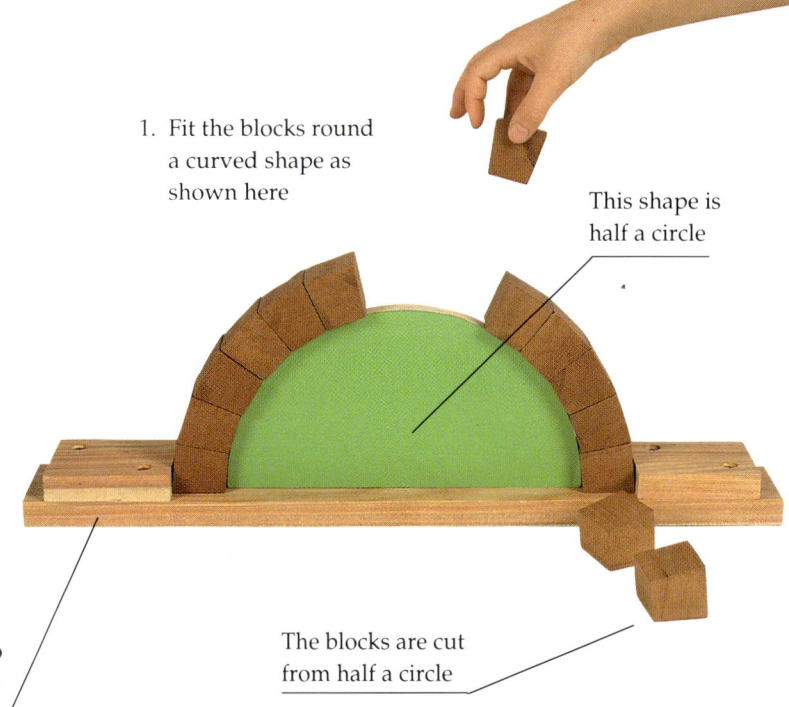

1. Fit the blocks round a curved shape as shown here

This shape is half a circle

The blocks are cut from half a circle

Arched over

To find out how an arch works use a sheet of cardboard bent into a curve and placed between two piles of heavy books.

Press down on the arch top and see what happens. If you put a piece of cardboard across the books, with it also resting on the top of the arch, you have made a very strong bridge like the one at Ironbridge.

Try making the arch with a lower curve and a higher curve. Do all shapes of arch work well?

The arch shown on the right has been made of blocks of wood. It shows how strong an arch can be even when it is made of separate pieces. If you want to try this experiment, ask a grown-up to cut some blocks of wood or polystyrene to the shapes shown here.

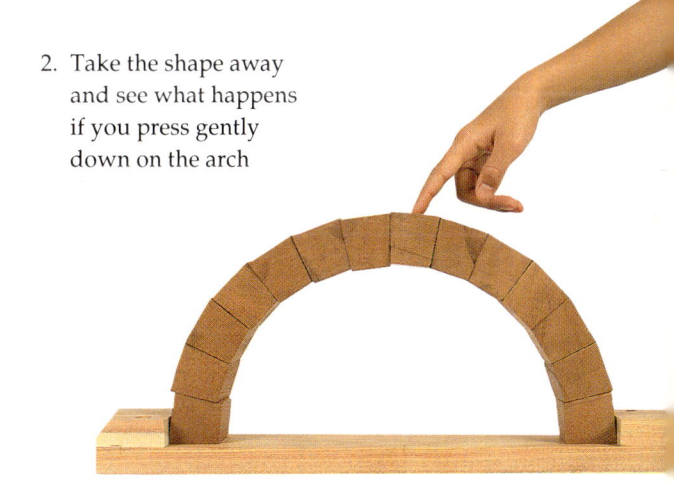

2. Take the shape away and see what happens if you press gently down on the arch

3. What happens when you press hard?

Columns

Rods can support enormous loads. The biggest rods are often found in buildings where they are called columns.

Nature also uses columns in the stems of plants.

Roof support
You can find out how many columns are needed to support a sheet of cardboard. Columns do not have to be round, they can be square, so you can use piles of building blocks.

Make some columns using single blocks and find out how many columns are needed to support the cardboard without it sagging.

Try various patterns of columns, such as placing them all round the edge of the cardboard sheet. Can you hold the cardboard up without any columns in the middle?

These columns are simply made of rolled up cardboard

Columns give space
Engineers sometimes use columns decoratively. The massive stone columns that hold up the roof of the Lincoln Memorial in the USA work just like a very thick wall, but they also let people see through to the inside of the building.

Giant trees
Trees are natural columns. As they grow upwards they also add to their thickness so they stay in proportion and the shape remains strong.

Trees can be of enormous size. The largest trees are the giant Sequoias of California. They are over 50 metres high and can be over 6 metres in diameter.

Trees are not rigid structures like stone columns, but they can give a little when there is a strong wind. Being **supple** therefore makes them even stronger.

Bars and beams

Bars and beams are horizontal structures. They hold up most of the floors in the world. You find beams in cranes and also in bridges. This is because beams are easy to make and use.

Nature uses few bars and beams because solid material is heavy and difficult to support.

Roads on stilts
Beams are commonly found in modern bridges and when engineers need to make raised roads.

The spacing of the stilts is decided by the strength of the beams. It would be possible to have much larger gaps between the stilts if arches were used, but beams are much cheaper to build.

Stone is a brittle material and easily snaps unless supported

How girders work
A simple bar is not a strong shape, but it can be strengthened easily by putting two bars together.

To see how easily a single bar bends you will need a piece of thin wood about the same shape as a wooden ruler. If you put it partly over the edge of a table and press, it will bend easily.

Now get a square section of wood and try bending this. Finally place the two bars together to make a girder shape. You will find that it is much more difficult to bend, yet the two pieces of wood use far less material than the solid piece of wood that would do the same job.

Stonehenge
Stonehenge is one of the ancient wonders of the world. But although it has lasted for thousands of years, it is not a strong shape.

The builders of Stonehenge could not have placed their pillars further apart or else the flat slabs on top would have snapped under their own weight.

Tubes and towers

If you take a flat sheet and curl it up on itself you have made a tube.

Because it gives a strong shape that is also light, tubes are used in many places where light weight is important. A lamp stand will be made from a tube and your bicycle frame is made up from tubes. A tall hollow building is often called a tower.

Framed
Bicycles are made of tubes because it is important to have a lightweight frame. All the pieces of tube are firmly fixed to make a rigid frame that will not twist.

The straws in the picture below show how, in principle, the tubes of the bicycle frame is also made of rigid triangles. Can you find the triangles on your bicycle?

This design stops the frame from changing shape when the rider's weight is added.

Bicycles in Amsterdam

Two triangular tubes make the famous 'diamond' shape of a bicycle frame

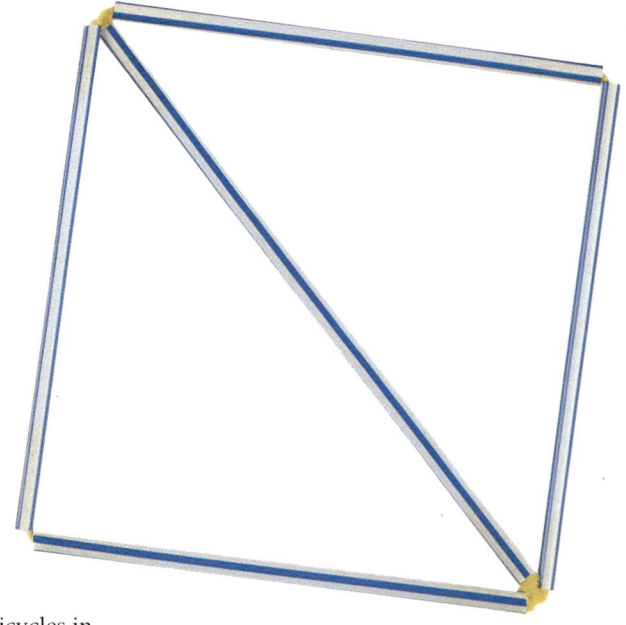

Paper chimney

You can see how even flimsy materials can be made strong by making them into tubes.

Take several sheets of newspaper and roll them together tightly. Use some adhesive tape to hold the outer sheet fast. Now carefully pull out the inner sheet. As it comes out twist it slightly to make a tighter tube – you will find it makes pulling easier.

See if you can pull out enough sheets to reach the ceiling and make a self-supporting chimney.

Tunnels

Tunnels are driven under mountains to make passes, under seas to connect countries and under cities to provide means of getting about.

All major tunnels are made as tubes (rather than arches) because they have to resist pressure from below as well as above. The tunnel shown in this picture was made as a tube and the lower part then filled in to make a roadway.

Towers

Some of the world's tallest structures are towers. All of them are hollow tubes, many with an elevator running up the centre.

The picture below shows the famous tower that houses Big Ben, the clock on the Houses of Parliament in London, England. This is a 'square tube'.

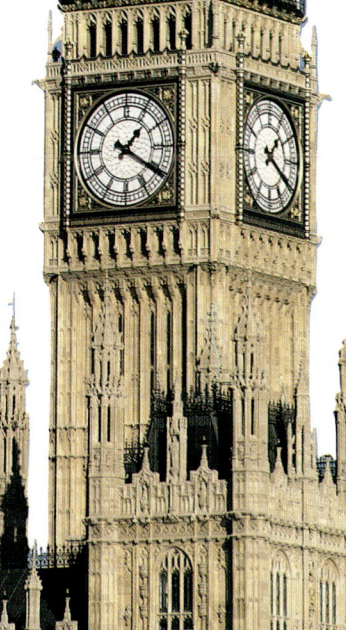

The Big Ben tower, at one end of London's Houses of Parliament

Hanging cables

The Brooklyn Bridge, New York

The Golden Gate Bridge spans the entrance to San Francisco harbour

A suspension bridge hangs on cables. It is a very important type of bridge because it can span great rivers or deep gorges without the need for supporting columns.

Suspending a bridge
First of all two large towers are built and the main cables hung so they form a natural curve.

The cables that hold the road or railway deck are now hung from the curve. The weight of the bridge deck is enough to keep the cables pulled tight.

Dancing cables

Spokes and cables are only strong when they are pulled tight. Suspension bridges depend on the weight of the deck to hold them tight.

But if the design is not right the bridge can begin to catch the wind and start to twist and turn.

The picture on the right shows the Tacoma Narrows (USA) bridge deck writhing about in a high wind and shaking itself to pieces.

Tight wires

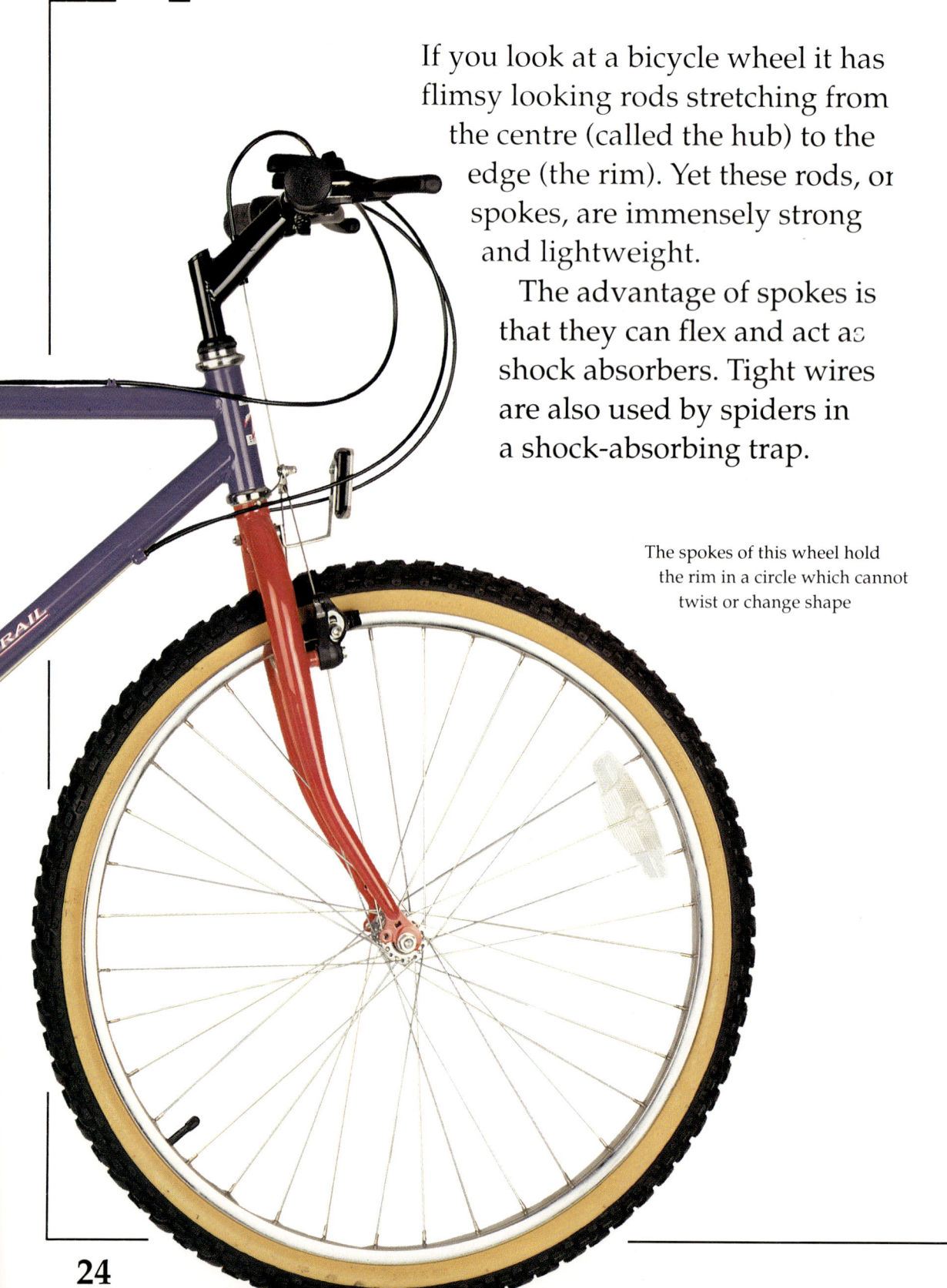

If you look at a bicycle wheel it has flimsy looking rods stretching from the centre (called the hub) to the edge (the rim). Yet these rods, or spokes, are immensely strong and lightweight.

The advantage of spokes is that they can flex and act as shock absorbers. Tight wires are also used by spiders in a shock-absorbing trap.

The spokes of this wheel hold the rim in a circle which cannot twist or change shape

Prove that spokes work
Rubber bands seem very weak and flimsy, but they can be made strong by turning them into spokes.

You can make a strong wheel using cardboard rings, a pencil and some large rubber bands. First cut two rings of cardboard like the ones shown here. Stick them together to stop the cardboard twisting.

Now, with the help of a friend, loop a rubber band round the pencil, over the cardboard rim and back under the pencil again.

At first the pencil will be dragged to one side of the rim, but as you add more bands and spread them out you will find the pencil is firmly held in the centre and you have a wheel with a hub. This is the principle of the bicycle wheel.

A spider in its web

Spider's web
The spider first makes a network of spokes and then ties them all together with a long spiral thread, working outwards from the centre.

When the web is complete it is a taut net. When an insect lands on it the vibrations of the web alert the spider and the spider can move in towards its prey.

25

Cones

Cones make sharp points and these can be used to force one shape into another. Many examples of cones can be found in nature. For example the teeth and claws of hunting animals are cone-shaped.

Make a cone from a circle
Cut out a circle in a piece of paper and then fold it in two so the halves exactly overlap. Make a crease and open the paper out again.

Cut along the crease right to the centre, then bring one part of the cut paper over the other. The farther you overlap the paper, the more pointed the cone will be.

You can fasten the cone with glue.

Now try pressing the paper cone against your skin. You will soon feel the sharp point of the cone because the force from your hand has all been concentrated at one point.

Nails
The point of a nail is cone-shaped and it is very effective at pushing wood aside and making room for the shaft of the nail.

Sharp claws
Many animals have claws that are cone-shaped. They have sharp points that stand out from a tough base. Claws have to be very strong because they are used to dig in and hold on.

An owl's claw

A shark's tooth

Teeth that hold fast
Many creatures that prey on others have sharp curving teeth. The front teeth of both dogs and cats curve backwards so they can hold on to their prey. They are also pointed to make the teeth cut into the prey more easily.

If you look closely at the shape of this shark's tooth you will see that teeth are only round and cone-shaped near the ends. They become more square shaped nearer the jaw. This shape stops the teeth from turning round in their sockets and gives greater pulling strength.

Dishes and domes

There are many dish and dome-shaped objects in our world. Some of the largest have been used as roofs, some of the smallest used as bowls and plates.

Dishes and domes are strong in two ways. You can push them from the inside or the outside and they still will keep their shape.

Designing dishes
You can look at some of the properties of a dish shape by cutting and sticking a flat piece of paper. First mark out a circle on a piece of paper, then cut out the circle and fold it over so the two halves overlap exactly. Make a crease along the fold. Fold the shape over on itself and make a crease again. The more times you fold and crease, the more guide lines you make and the closer you will get to a true dish shape.

Cut a slit along each fold until you nearly reach the centre. Draw one side of each slit over the next by an equal amount. Use glue to fix the overlaps in place.

Notice that less material is used in the dish than in the flat sheet.

Domes spread the strain
The picture on the right shows the white marble domes of the Taj Mahal, India, one of the most famous domed buildings in the world.

A dome works like an arch. The greater its weight, the more the dome building blocks are pressed firmly together.

The bottom edge of the dome is upright, and this means the roof is easily supported on the walls of the building.

A dish shape is used to protect this terrapin from attackers

Strong and safe
Domes are one of the strongest shapes. If the surface of a dome is knocked the shock will be **absorbed** by the whole dome. This is the reason people wear domed safety hats when they are in places where falling things might cause head injury. Inside the hard hat there is a shock-absorbing cage that fits over the head.

Spheres

Balls are round in every direction – a shape called a sphere. There is no weak point to a sphere. Everywhere it curves out towards you. This is what makes a sphere the strongest shape of all.

Joints on the move
All animals have special joints to help them move. You can examine one of these joints by looking at the bones of a chicken leg after the meat has been eaten.

You will see that joint has shaped bones that make a ball and socket. This allows the joint to be moved in any direction.

Between the joints is a white rubbery sheet – called **cartilage**. Without cartilage the bones would grind against each other and wear away.

On the rebound
A tennis ball shows the properties of a ball well. It does not matter which way you try to squash it, it will always spring back to a sphere.

Bearing up
Spheres are used in many places when we want something to move easily. There is a metal ball in the end of a ball-point pen. Look closely and you will see the ball.

There are also balls in many machines such as bicycles. These balls are kept in a casing round the wheel spindle. As the wheel turns the spindle turns against the ball bearings, making it smooth running.

These are the bread boards used to make the bearing. They are round with a groove cut in one side. The marbles fit in the groove

Bearing marbles
Find out about the use of balls as strong shapes that can move heavy weights.

You need two boards of the kind used for cutting bread or two shallow trays.

Place marbles on the groove of one board until no more will fit. Place the other board upside down in the first. This makes a **bearing**.

Try moving the bearing about. It should move easily clockwise or anticlockwise. Put a heavy weight, such as a book, on the dish. Find out if the bearings still work well.

Does it matter if you have many marbles, or just a few?

31

Shells

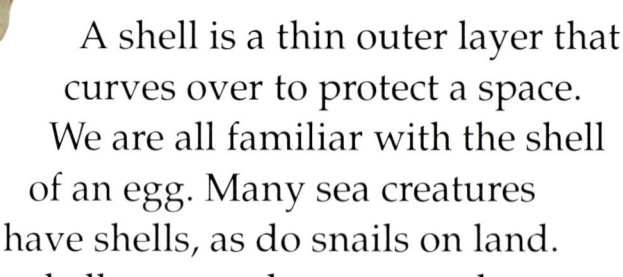

A shell is a thin outer layer that curves over to protect a space. We are all familiar with the shell of an egg. Many sea creatures have shells, as do snails on land. As shells are used to protect the things inside, they have to be strong. Some live in the deep oceans and can stand up to huge pressures of water. It is all a matter of curves.

Secrets of the sea shell

Sea shells are the homes to many creatures and come in many shapes and sizes. The one on the left is the shell of a whelk. The ball-shaped 'shells' in the pictures below belong to sea urchins. Although we call them shells they are actually the skeletons of the animals. They use the ball shape to protect and support their soft inner parts.

Mussels, clams and many similar animals have two shells – like two cups put open ends together. They open up when the animals need to feed.

32

Light bulbs

A light bulb or a television tube is a shell of thin glass, yet it is very strong.

Light bulbs work when electricity passes through a fine wire. In air the fine wire would burn up, so it is put in a glass bulb with a special gas at low pressure.

Using a sphere makes it possible to use thin glass without fear of it crushing under the pressure of the outside air.

These spheres hold gases under pressure

An ostrich's egg

Eggseptional

Find out about the properties of an egg. Use a chicken's egg bought from a store and place it on a kitchen scale. Now place a cake tin or other hard strong surface on the egg and see how much pressure you have to apply before the egg breaks.

A hen's egg

It is best to do egg experiments just before a grown-up is about to start cooking. Then the broken eggs won't go to waste

33

Getting support

Shapes have to serve a purpose. A shelf, for example, has to be wide and flat.

To make useful shapes into even stronger shapes supports are used. We have seen columns used in this way on page 16.

Many other kinds of support use angled bars and wires.

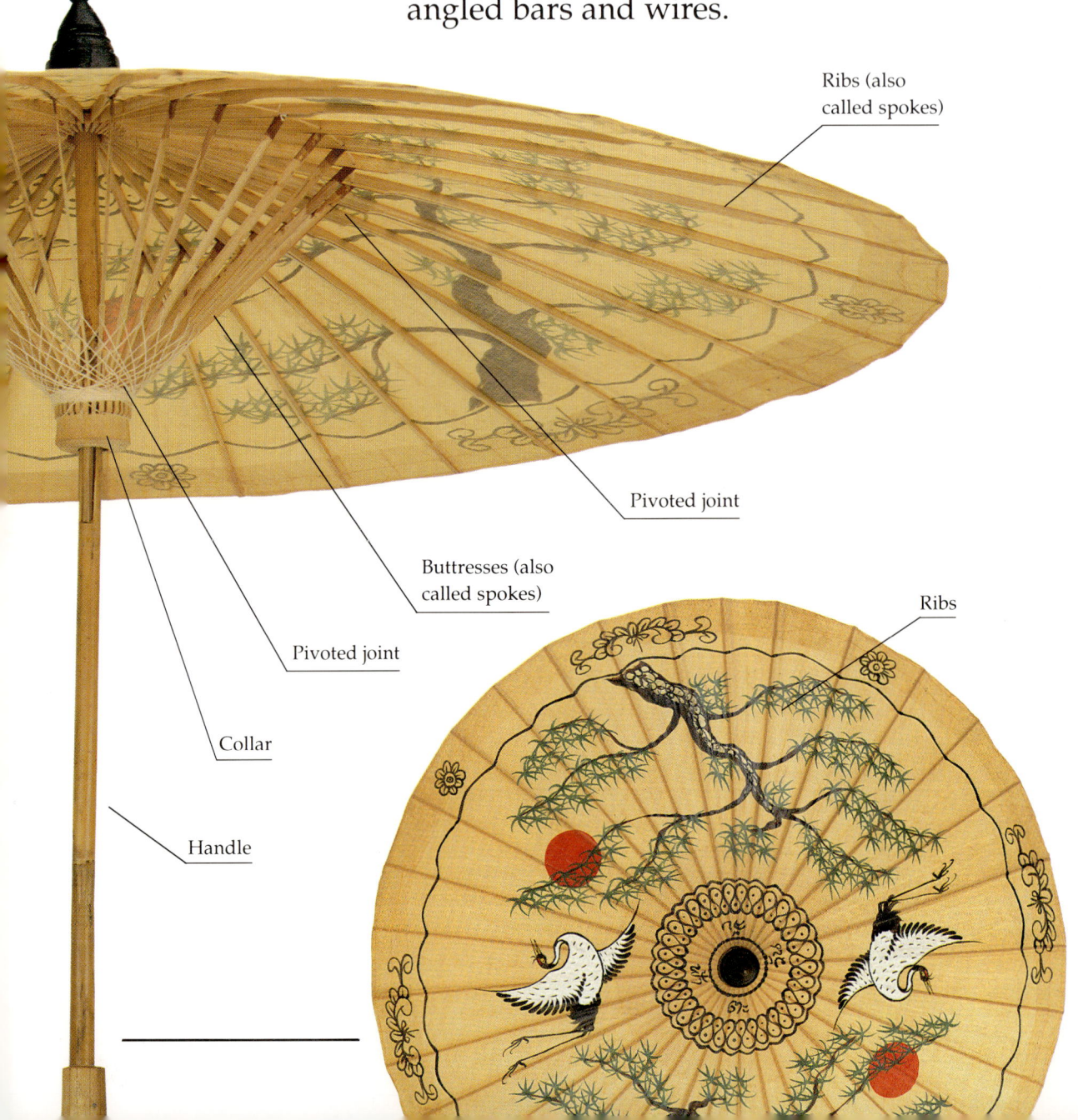

Ribs (also called spokes)

Pivoted joint

Buttresses (also called spokes)

Ribs

Pivoted joint

Collar

Handle

This modern cathedral is built like a crown. It uses buttresses as part of the design as well as to give a strong shape

House of cards
If you make a house from playing cards you can see why the walls need support.

Very carefully make a house using three cards. It is a flat roofed house.

Make the house on a cloth surface so the cards won't slip. Now very gently push down on the 'roof' card and watch the 'walls'. The place where the walls first begin to move is the place to give support.

A lightweight problem
An umbrella is made of lightweight materials so it can be easily carried about. The umbrella shown in the pictures on the left was made in Thailand from waxed and painted paper.

To make the umbrella usable the fabric surface must become taut when it is opened. This is done by giving support to the fabric using many ribs.

The ribs on these umbrellas are made of thin bamboo, and they must be held up strongly. Each rib is given its own buttress. When the umbrella is opened the buttresses are forced out and they lift the ribs into place. The buttresses and ribs are kept taut and the shape made strong by the collar and clip on the umbrella handle.

All umbrellas work in the same way. Notice that the umbrella has buttresses which are **pivoted** at each end. This allows the umbrella to be opened and closed with ease.

Propping up walls
The weight of a heavy roof on a high wall may cause the wall to buckle out and the building to fall down, just like a house of cards.

To prevent the wall collapsing it can be supported by a prop called a buttress. Quite often a buttress is covered up and made to look like a decoration.

A buttress (in blue and red) is used to hold up a wall (in yellow)

35

How frames work

Making something completely out of solid materials can be wasteful. Very often a frame will work just as well.

One of the simplest frames is a ladder. Here two long bars are kept an even distance apart by many short bars (the steps).

Engineers often use triangles as the shapes for their frames.

Making a strong frame
Strong frames must not change shape when a force is added. A common force is the weight of the walls and roof of a house.

A triangle is the only shape that cannot be altered, because the three lengths will only make one shape. This is why it is used in many structures. You can find triangles in the frame that is being made over this shopping mall, and there are many triangles in the frame of the Eiffel Tower (right) the famous iron monument in Paris, France.

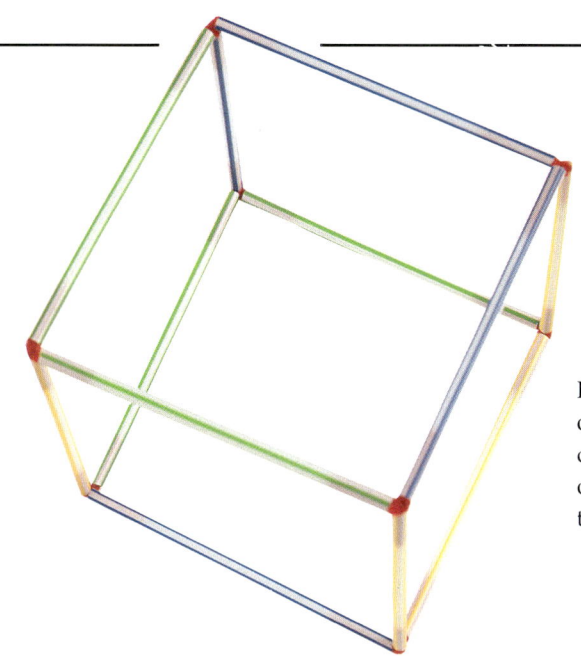

A diagonal goes between opposite corners

If you push the frame on the left it will change shape to the one below. It needs to be strengthened

Well framed?

A frame only works if it can be made into a rigid shape. You can see the problems by using straws and pipe cleaners to make a square frame – a cube.

Begin by tying four straws of equal length together at each corner using pieces of pipe cleaners.

If you have had to pull or push the straws into shape you will already have discovered that four tubes make all sorts of four-sided shapes in addition to a cube.

Cut and tie another straw from one corner to another to make a diagonal. It will need to be longer than the straws that made the sides of the frame. Experiment to get the right length. Some diagonals will make the frame stronger than others. Which are they? Could such diagonals be placed easily in a real building?

A scaffolding frame

37

Nests

The nest is attached to a twig on a tree by weaving grasses round it and making a knot

Many animals build nests. Remember that these animals have to do their best with what nature provides. Most have to build with claws, teeth or beaks: they don't have hands or machinery like us. Discover what marvellous feats of engineering they are able to achieve.

High level weaver

Many birds make nests from grass, twigs, mosses and leaves that lie loose on the ground. Most nests also have to be built high off the ground for protection.
This is the nest of a weaver bird from Africa. It is made with dried grasses that have been worked with the bird's beak. Each grass stem is pushed between, or woven, in with the others. In this way the bird makes a lightweight frame without any nuts or bolts!

The nest is woven using grasses. Younger birds do not always make a satisfactory shape first time: a few tries may be needed

The bird enters its nest from below through this woven entrance tube

This termitarium is nearly 3 metres high. It also extends about 2 metres below ground.

It has two tall chimneys and several chimneys nearer the ground

Termite city

Termites are small ant-like insects found in areas of the world that have a long warm dry season each year.

Termites make a nest deep underground for their queen to lay her eggs. She, and her eggs need to be kept cool.

The worker termites build tall chimneys out of mud to provide a type of air conditioning. One or more chimneys are taller than the others. As the wind flows round the tall chimneys it sucks out the hot stale air from the tunnels of the nest, while cooler, fresh air flows in through the lower chimneys.

Packed together

Shapes are often strongest when they fit together well. The largest number of sides that will fit together without leaving gaps is six.

A common example of a six-sided strong shape is a honeycomb. But bees are not alone in needing to pack shapes together.

A wild bees' nest in the crook of a tree

A honeycomb oozing honey

Bees home
The bees make six-sided homes, the honeycomb, for **larvae** by spitting out wax and working it with their jaws.

In nature the bees make nests in trees and they have to build a nest that will hang up, yet will hold thousands of eggs.

The secret has been to make the nest out of six-sided compartments called **cells**. To make the nest bigger, the bees just weld a new cell alongside another one.

Getting the light
Trees use their leaves to gather sunlight. But the Sun is constantly moving across the sky. To cope with this problem many trees fan the leaves out in every direction by using a complicated pattern of branches and twigs.

Look at a tree and see how evenly the leaves cover the canopy of the tree. Although the leaves are packed together closely, few of them get in one another's way.

Egg boxes
Eggs need to be carried from the farm to the shop and then to homes. Eggs would soon become crushed if they were not packed into a protective box. Egg boxes are often built with cells that are honeycomb shaped.

Corals build their own props
Coral reefs are made from the work of millions of tiny animals. The hard coral **polyps** build a six ribbed skeleton and live in large colonies which form coral reefs.

Corals need to pack densely for protection, but they also need water to flow past them so they can gather food. To achieve this they build an even spacing of finger-like structures called 'branches'.

This piece of dead coral shows the structure clearly. The world's greatest coral reef is the Great Barrier Reef of Australia

41

Skyscrapers

A skyscraper is a wonder of engineering.

A skyscraper has to be strong enough to support its own huge weight. It has to withstand the sideways force of storm force winds and even the shaking force of earthquakes. And it has to have plenty of space inside for people to work and live.

All of this is only possible because frames give strong, lightweight shapes.

Shake-proof
This building fell down during an **earthquake** because it did not have a frame that could stand up to ground shaking.

Taking the weight
In a modern skyscraper the strength is in the steel frame. The floors and the walls are hung from the frame. This means that the walls can be made of lightweight materials because they do not carry any load.

In the right hand building in the picture above the frame can clearly be seen. When it is complete it will have walls that will hide the frame just like the one on the left.

42

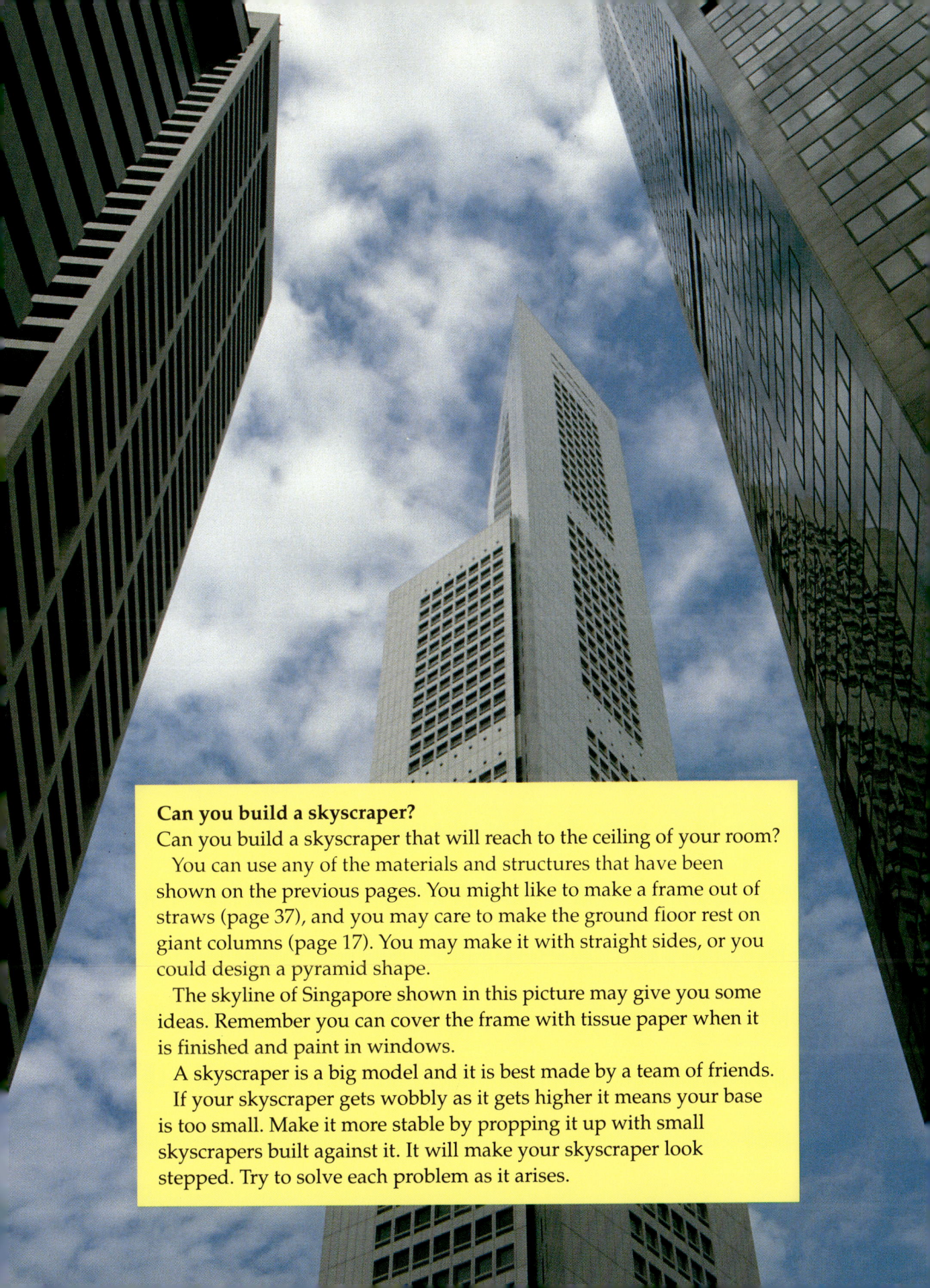

Can you build a skyscraper?
Can you build a skyscraper that will reach to the ceiling of your room?

You can use any of the materials and structures that have been shown on the previous pages. You might like to make a frame out of straws (page 37), and you may care to make the ground floor rest on giant columns (page 17). You may make it with straight sides, or you could design a pyramid shape.

The skyline of Singapore shown in this picture may give you some ideas. Remember you can cover the frame with tissue paper when it is finished and paint in windows.

A skyscraper is a big model and it is best made by a team of friends.

If your skyscraper gets wobbly as it gets higher it means your base is too small. Make it more stable by propping it up with small skyscrapers built against it. It will make your skyscraper look stepped. Try to solve each problem as it arises.

Our strong shapes

Living is full of hazards. To cope with this all living creatures have to be made of strong shapes. You can see this most easily by looking at skeletons.

On this page you will see parts of a human skeleton. Each part is made up of many strong shapes. Some of them have been pointed out for you.

Look carefully and see how many other strong shapes you can find – and why each part is shaped the way it is.

Hands

Hands are made of many small bones. They have to be able to move easily and quickly in many directions.

Look at this picture and compare it with your hand. Notice how the set of hand bones nearest the wrist are entirely enclosed by skin to make the palm.

Move your hand about and wiggle your fingers and wrist. Find out what each of your joints does and how this matches the type of joint you see.

Bones are wider at the joints. This gives a bigger and therefore stronger area where the biggest forces are found

These joints are designed to move in only one direction. Notice how the joints fit together to stop a sideways movement

Spine
Our spine carries all the weight of our upper body. See how the bones are thick. None of the bones has a true ball or socket. Bend your back and see how much movement there is. The effect of many small bones moving just a little is to spread the pressure and give a very strong bendy shape

Pelvis
The lower part of your skeleton is called the pelvis and many other bones are fixed to it.

Half of the pelvis is shown here. Notice that is made like a broad blade, but it is curved for greater strength

Note: There is a shock-absorbing material called cartilage between each pair of moving bones to stop them grinding together as they move.

Hip joint
Your hip contains a true ball and socket joint (another is in your shoulder)

This means the leg can be swung in every direction.

The ball and socket are large because they have to take the whole weight of your upper body

Ribs
Feel your ribs to see how they are bones that form a cage to protect your heart and lungs. See how it resembles a ladder frame. The curve of each bone gives it strength and flexibility. This allows them to take small shocks without breaking.

Legs
Leg bones have to carry the whole weight of our bodies and are therefore thicker and stronger than the arm bones

New words

absorb
to soak up. Rubber is an example of a material that changes shape and absorbs pulls and pushes

bearing
a support for a moving part. The hub of a bicycle wheel contains a bearing. This allows the heel to turn easily on the shaft

cartilage
the rubbery layer of tissue – often known as gristle – that grows between moving bones and which acts as a combined bearing and shock-absorber

cell
a closed shape that packs together with other similar shapes to form a pattern. In a honeycomb made by bees each cell is made of wax and is occupied by an egg

cone
a shape with a circular base and sloping sides that meet at a point. A wizard's hat is often shown as a tall cone in books

corrugation
a surface that is shaped into long lines of wrinkles. Corrugations are often added to materials to make them stronger. Sheets of wrapping paper and sheets of steel (intended for use as roofing) are common examples

cylinder
a solid shape with a circular plan. Rods, columns and trees are all examples of cylinders. A hollow cylinder is called a tube

earthquake
violent shaking of the ground due to great movements deep within the Earth. An earthquake can cause enough damage to buildings to make them collapse

force
The effort that is applied on an object. There are many different ways of creating a force. Pushing this book so that it moves is an example of a force

key stones
the centre stone of an arch made of blocks. Key stones are wedge-shaped so that they will fit round a curve

larva
an immature form of many animals. A caterpillar is an example of a larva. When it has grown through the first stage, the larva spins itself a cocoon and there is slowly changes form, eventually emerging as a butterfly or moth

mortar
a mixture of cement and sand and lime that makes a fine paste suitable for cementing building blocks together

nectar
a sugary solution produced by many flowers and which attracts insects, birds or bats. As the animal sips the nectar it brushes against the flower, bringing in pollen to fertilise the plant and taking more pollen away to fertilise other plants

pier
a thickened piece of a wall designed to give strength and to stop the wall from falling over

pivot
the point about which something turns. A door, for example, pivots about its hinges

polyp
an animal with a hollow cylindrical body with tentacles round the mouth. Many coral animals are polyps. They make a finned chalky frame as they grow. This remains after the animal has died and becomes a permanent part of a coral reef

pyramid
a shape with a square base and four sloping triangular sides that meet in a point. The most famous examples of a pyramid are the Pyramids of Giza, huge burial chambers of the ancient Egyptian kings or pharaohs

rectangle
a square shape with all edges at right angles. However, unlike squares, rectangles do not have all edges the same length. A square is a special form of a rectangle

rod
any slim cylinder of material giving it a stick-like shape

skyscraper
a building used as apartments or offices, which is unusually tall and which is made with a frame to hold it up

sphere
a ball-shaped object. Spheres roll easily in any direction and they are used in many bearings

supple
a material that is supple can bend easily without damage. The new shoots on a tree are very supple and will bend over on themselves without breaking, yet they can also stand up straight when no force is applied

Index

absorb 29, 46
arch 15

ball 30
bamboo 11, 35
bar 18
beam 18
bearing 31, 46
bicycle 21, 24,
block 8, 9
bone 30, 44
branch 41
brick 8
bridge 14, 22
buttress 34

cacti 12
can 12
cartilage 30, 45, 46
cell 40, 46
chimney 39
chisel 7
claw 27
column 16, 17
cone 5, 26, 46
container 8
coral reef 41
corrugation 12, 46
crinkles 12
crushing 32
curve 10, 14
curve popping 10
cylinder 4, 16, 20, 46

dish 28
dome 28, 29
door stop 7

earthquake 42, 46
egg 32, 33, 40

force 6, 46
frame 21, 36

girders 19

hands 44
hanging cables 22
hard hat 29
hip 45
honeycomb 40
hub 24

Indonesia 11

joint 30
joints 44

key stones 15, 46

ladder 36
larva 40, 46
leaves 41
leg 45
light bulb 32

marbles 31
mortar 9, 47

nail 26
natural stone arch 14
nectar 11, 47
nest 38

packing 40
pelvis 45
petal 11

pier 9, 47
pillar 19
pivot 35, 47
polyp 41, 47
pyramid 4, 6, 47

rectangle 4, 8, 47
ribs 35, 45
rod 4, 16, 47
roofs 11, 16

saguaro cactus 12
sea urchin 33
shark 27
shells 13, 32
skeleton 44
skyscraper 6, 42, 47
sphere 4, 29, 30, 47
spider's web 25
spine 45
spokes 23, 24, 25
steel frame 42
supple 17, 47
suspension bridge 22

taper 6
teeth 27
tennis ball 30
termites 39
tree 17, 41
triangle 6, 36
tube 20
tunnel 21

umbrella 35

wall 9
weaving 38
wedge 6, 7

48